Water

Sally Hewitt

W

FRANKLIN WATTS
LONDON•SYDNEY

This editon 2011
First published by Franklin Watts
338 Euston Road
London NW1 3BH

Franklin Watts Australia
Level 17/207 Kent Street
Sydney NSW 2000
Copyright © Franklin Watts 2008

Editor: Jeremy Smith
Art director: Jonathan Hair
Design: Jason Anscomb

We would like to thank Berkswich Primary School, Del Prado Elementary School,
London Wetlands Centre, Shree Padre, Southfields Primary School, Unicef and
Kathleen Janatik for the case studies supplied for this book.

Picture credits: Alamy 3, 5, 6, 8 all. 9tr, 22, 24, 25 all. Berkswich Primary School: 15c.
Corbis: 12 all. Del Prado Elementary School: 19 all, istockphoto: 6bl, 9tl, 23 all.
Kathleen Janatik: 17 all. London Wetlands Centre: 18 all. Shree Padre: 13 all. Shutterstock:14 all,
16 all. Southfields Primary School: 11 all. Unicef: 27. Web Aviation Images: 7br.

Every effort has been made to clear copyright. Should there be any inadvertant omission,
please contact the publisher for rectification.

Dewey Classification: 941.085
ISBN: 978 1 4451 0601 4

Printed in China

Franklin Watts is a division of Hachette Children's
Books, an Hachette UK company.
www.hachette.co.uk

Contents

A world of water

Over 70 per cent of our planet Earth is covered by seas and oceans.
That is a great deal of water! But of all the water on Earth, only
2 per cent is fresh water we can drink and most of that is locked up
as ice. The other 98 per cent is salty sea water.

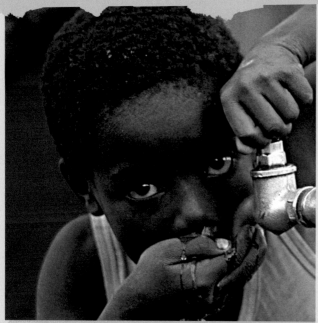

All living things depend on water to stay alive and keep healthy. To be a member of the Green Team, we need to look after every drop of our precious water.

Water cycle

There are no new supplies of water. The water we drink today was around in the time of the dinosaurs. Water goes round and round in a cycle. 1. Most rain falls on the seas, oceans, rivers and lakes. About a fifth falls on land, and part of this will find its way back into rivers and then into the sea. 2. Plants use up some water, and release some back into the air. 3. The sun warms surface water (on land and on the oceans), which evaporates, forming clouds. 4. Water eventually falls from these clouds as rain.

The same water falls on Earth as rain billions of times, over and over again.

Challenge!

Write down all the different things you use water for at home every day.

For example:
- drinking
- cleaning teeth
- flushing the toilet.

Imagine what life would be like if clean water didn't flow through your tap and was difficult to get hold of.

Different types of water

Salt water

The water in seas and oceans is salt water. We can't drink salt water but it is an important part of the water cycle that gives us fresh water to drink (see page 6). We need to keep it free of pollution to help the whole planet to stay healthy.

Fresh water

Water in rivers and lakes and underground water is called fresh water because it isn't salty. Animals and plants that live on land depend on fresh water for life. We need to look after our fresh water, keep it clean and not waste it.

Rain

Rain doesn't fall evenly all over the world. Some parts of the world get more rain than others. Rainforests, where rain falls every day, are teeming with life. Deserts get hardly any rain and so only a few plants and animals can survive there.

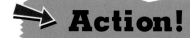

Action!

Water is vital for life. We must not waste it.

You can save 4.5 litres of clean, fresh, drinking water a day! It's as easy as turning off the tap when you clean your teeth.

Climate change

Climate is the kind of weather a place has over a long period of time. There are signs that the climate is changing all over the world. Patterns of rainfall and temperature are changing and there are more storms, droughts and floods. These affect our fresh water supplies. Scientists think this climate change is partly caused by the way we live today. The Green Team can try to do something about climate change.

Climate change is causing more droughts in Africa (below left). Wells dry up and food crops die. In other parts of the world such as Britain (below right), flooding is becoming more common.

Every drop counts

Every year, the number of people on Earth grows, but the amount of water stays the same. With more people on Earth needing water to drink and for washing, and more factories using water, demands on precious water grow all the time, so every drop counts!

Leaks

Water escapes from leaks in water pipes and from dripping taps. Water can be saved when water companies repair damaged pipes. We can make sure that leaks are mended at home.

Wasting water

It costs money and uses energy to collect, clean and pump water into our homes (see page 10). We use this water not just for drinking, but also for washing, cooking, cleaning and watering the garden. When we have finished with it, we pour it down the drain or flush it down the toilet.

When water is scarce, people use far less water. These people in Zimbabwe have to extract water from the ground using a water pump. They use the water they can get carefully.

In richer countries, people use about 150 litres of clean, fresh water every day. That's 150 bottles of water like this.

Challenge!

Think about the different ways you use water at home and at school.

- Does water have to be clean and fresh for everything?
- What do you do with water when you have used it?
- Could you use the same water more than once?
- Do you waste water?

Just making sure the tap isn't dripping can save 4 litres of water per day. That's 1,460 litres a year!

Save water at home

We waste water in our homes every day. There are things you can do that will save precious water and save you money.

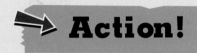 **Action!**

Save water.

- Turn off dripping taps.
- Take a short shower instead of a bath.
- Turn off the tap while you are cleaning your teeth.
- Wash your hands in a small amount of water in the basin with the plug in.
- Use a bowl for washing-up, not running water.
- Only run your washing machine and dishwasher with full loads.
- Don't run water until it is cold for a drink. Put a jug of water in the fridge.

What other water-saving ideas can you think of?

Green Team action!

Wes, Amy, Nirmal, Paul and Lei are members of their school Green Team. They want to save water at school.

First they need to set up a committee of pupils and staff to get action going. The next step is to have a water survey to check how the school uses water. Then they need some water-saving ideas and to make an action plan. Regular checks will make sure things get done.

Save Our Water!

More and more ice is melting. More people need to turn taps off.

Green Team members designed a poster to promote saving water. You could do the same.

Clean water

When we turn on the tap, clean water pours out. When we have used it, we pour it down the sink, down the drain or flush it away. It goes through pipes back to the water company, who clean it again and pipe it back to us. In many places in the world, clean water is difficult to find, however.

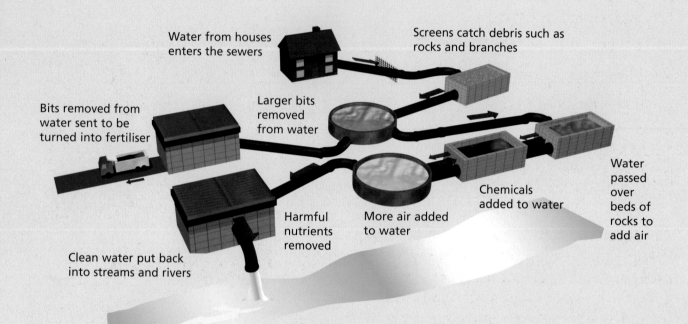

Water from houses enters the sewers

Screens catch debris such as rocks and branches

Bits removed from water sent to be turned into fertiliser

Larger bits removed from water

Water passed over beds of rocks to add air

Chemicals added to water

More air added to water

Harmful nutrients removed

Clean water put back into streams and rivers

Water from sinks and drains is cleaned at a water treatment works. Water from the toilet goes to the sewage treatment works. It takes energy and money to clean water.

Down the drain

It's easy to pour away things other than water without thinking. But we should ask ourselves, "Is this a good idea?" Oil doesn't mix with or dissolve in water. It forms a film and is very difficult to get rid of. If oil gets into the sea and rivers, it causes pollution and harms wildlife. Let cooking oil turn solid or put it into a container before putting it in the rubbish, not the sink.

Keeping healthy

Clean water is essential for keeping healthy. Dirty water is full of germs that can make us sick. Where there is no clean water, people, particularly children, suffer.

Challenge!

Find out what is poured down the drain at home and at school.

Make sure oil and chemicals are disposed of properly and never poured down the drain.

Case study – Southfields Primary and Nyogbare School

The children of Southfields Primary School, Coventry, exchanged postcards with Nyogbare School in Ghana. The children of Southfields Primary wrote about graffiti while the children of Nyogbare School wrote about the problems they face because of a lack of clean water.

Southfields pupils contacted the charity Water Aid who responded by digging a deep bore hole, bringing clean, fresh water to the Ghanean school and the local community. The Southfields deputy head, Margaret Hope, travelled to Ghana to see the project for herself. Nyogbare's principal, Jacob Tibil, has visited Southfields Primary in return.

The deputy at Southfields Primary, Margaret Hope (below), says:

"The power of young people's voices, in both the south and the north, got the bore hole made, and both schools were active partners in this development."

➤ Action!

Get involved and support a charity such as Water Aid.

This charity works with communities all over the world to set up clean water supplies.

Southfields' pupil Ian, 10, said:

"Now that Jacob has been to stay with us, the children at Nyogbare feel like close friends. It's great that they told us about the problem and we have been able to help."

Reusing water

One of the best ways of saving water is to use it twice. Some of your school and household water can be used again before it is poured away.

Black water

Water from the toilet is called black water. It is sent to a sewage treatment works. Black water has to be treated and cleaned before it is used again because it is full of germs.

Grey water

Grey water is the name for household water from the bath, shower, washing machine and dishwasher. Rainwater is also a type of grey water. It can be used again if you have a grey water system fitted at home or at school. Instead of being poured away, grey water is piped to a collection tank and reused to flush the toilets or water the garden. Any grey water not used within a day is pumped away.

Using water again helps to save precious clean water. Here, people are examining a grey water tank at a green fair in Montana, USA.

If you don't add bubble bath to your bath water you will be able to use it again.

If you reuse grey water without a grey water system, make sure it is filtered first to remove any solids, then add a little bleach to disinfect it. Allow it to settle for a few days before using the water.

Challenge!

Reuse your bath water.

- A watering can of bath water can be used to water your garden.
- A bucket of bath water can be used to clean the car or the windows.

Case study – Reusing water in India

In areas with little rain, reusing grey water at school makes sense. At the Neernalli Madhyamika Shikshanalaya School in Uttara Karnataka, southern India, a rain centre has been set up. Students and the general public are taught about how to save rainwater

Madhyamika Shikshanalaya High School runs water conservation classes for the whole region.

A student inspects a newly installed ground water tank that collects run-off rain water.

and how to use grey water. There are 28 different ways to save water on display around the school, from tanks that can collect grey water from rooftops, to groundwater tanks that collect run-off grey water.

M S Hegde, chairman of the water project at the school, says:

"We need to make serious efforts to educate our people, be they urban or rural. After all, nobody can live without water. Our rain centre is the result of three years' preparation."

Action!

Reuse water at school.

- Collect water from lunch jugs and mugs and use it to water plants and the school garden.
- Find out if your school grey water can be reused.
- Ask your school to apply to your local council for a grant to set up a grey water system.

Rainwater

Rainwater is fresh water. We can use it for drinking, cooking and washing. Collecting rainwater instead of tap water and using it for watering the garden or cleaning helps us to make the most of every drop.

Collecting rainwater

On the small, crowded island of Bermuda, surrounded by the Atlantic Ocean, there are no lakes or rivers to provide fresh water to drink. People rely on rainwater to seep into underground pools and fill water tanks. Every home must collect rain from the roof, and store it in a tank.

Roofs in Bermuda are scrubbed clean and painted white to keep the rain clean. The roofs are sloping to collect as much rainfall as possible.

Warning! Never drink fresh rainwater!

Water butts

Water butts are big barrels for collecting rainwater that falls on the roof. They can be installed at home or at school. Rain falls and rolls down a sloping roof into a gutter, which slopes towards a down pipe. The rain is collected in a water butt at the bottom of the pipe.

During 2007, Dublin City Council in Ireland gave all schools in Dublin water butts (above) for use in school gardens. Schools were also given "hippo bags" to put in toilet cisterns. These reduce the amount of water used every time a toilet is flushed.

Challenge!

Collect rainwater and help to save the environment.

- Leave out a bucket to collect rainwater to water your garden, plants in containers and houseplants.
- Get a water butt installed at home or at school to collect and use rainwater.

Case study – Berkswich Primary School

Berkswich Primary School, in the UK, have created an environment centre from a weedy, run-down courtyard. This area often flooded and was an eyesore. The area now grows produce for the school kitchen and features an outside classroom for the children to work in. Pupils have created a weather station that helps them to track climate change and links them with schools all over the world via the Internet. Rainfall is monitored and collected to use on the garden plants. The project aims to recycle 22,000 litres of rainwater every year.

In the outside classroom at Berkswich Primary School, vegetables are grown using rainwater.

Alison, a student at Berkswich Primary, says:

"It's amazing how much water comes off our school roof and is wasted. After a short rain shower, we have enough water in our collection tanks to last us a week in our school garden and it's free!"

Action!

Make a rain gauge.

You will need

- Clear plastic ruler
- Clear jar
- Rubber band
- Funnel
- Transparent tape

Instructions

1. Remove the jar's label.
2. Attach the ruler to the outside of the jar with the rubber band. Tape the ruler in place so the numbers can be read from the outside of the jar.
3. Place the funnel in the top of the jar. The top end of the funnel should cover the entire mouth of the jar.
4. Put the jar out in the rain, not too near to trees or too close to buildings which may block the rain.
5. Read the ruler to determine how much rain was collected in a set amount of time.
6. Empty the jar after each use.

Living water

Rivers, streams, reservoirs and lakes provide us with fresh water. They are home to all kinds of animals and plants. Green Team members help to keep local water clean and healthy for all the life that depends on it.

Water pollution

You can spot signs that water is not clean and healthy. Litter, such as cans, bottles and plastic bags, blocks the water flow and is harmful to wildlife. Certain types of plants growing in the water, and algae covering the water surface, are a sign of fertilisers or sewage in the water. They block out the light and kill other plants and water animals through lack of oxygen. A shiny slick of oil on the surface will coat water birds and kill them. Foam and bubbles in the water can be a sign of pollution from soap, detergents and other chemicals.

Herons on the banks are a sign of a healthy river. They catch and eat fish that live in clean, running water.

Clean, healthy water is full of plants and wildlife. It is safe for everyone to enjoy.

Challenge!

Get to know your local water.

- Visit a local river, stream, reservoir or lake with an adult. Does it look clean and fresh?
- What birds, insects and mammals can you spot living there?
- What plants are growing?
- Is the water clean and litter free?
- Are people walking, boating, fishing and enjoying the water?

⇒ Action!

The Green Team can help to keep rivers and streams clean and fresh.

- Clean up after your dog when you are out for a walk.
- Put litter in the bin.
- Keep the area outside your house free of leaves, grass clippings or anything that might wash down the drain in the street.
- Ask your parents to make sure the car isn't leaking oil, which could run down the drain and into the water system.

A student from Knapp Elementary School in Michigan City, USA, tests a water sample.

How does pollution happen?

Water becomes polluted when heavy rainfall washes dirt from the streets, including dog poo, down the drain and into the local water. In addition, power stations pump out dirty water and factories leak chemicals. We throw litter into the water and boats leak oil.

Case study – World Water Monitoring Day

World Water Monitoring Day (WWMD) is a global event that teaches schoolchildren about the water around them and their responsibility to look after it.

Fourth-graders at Knapp Elementary School in Michigan City, USA, monitored water quality during a field trip with the help of Michigan City Sanitary District Chemist, Kathleen Janatik. A learning

lab was set up, where pupils learnt about the water cycle, water conservation, wastewater, and the animals that live in this habitat. Each student collected water samples and tested them in the lab, logging their findings in their WWMD kit booklets.

Karen Franz, Watershed Monitoring Program Director, says:

"World Water Monitoring Day allows students to join together and take a hands-on approach to understanding the value of clean water for people, plants and wildlife. The data collected today is shared with other students around the world – illustrating that this is an issue of international significance for which we are all responsible."

Local water

Wherever you live, there will probably be some kind of water – a stream, a pond, a river, a lake or the sea. Every piece of water supports plants and wildlife. Green Team members get involved and help to look after their local water.

Uncared-for water

Water that is uncared for creates problems for the local area. Blocked waterways cause flooding and endanger homes. Polluted water can kill wildlife and plants and contaminate the water supply. Overgrown and neglected waterways become dirty and dangerous places to visit instead of pleasant places to walk.

Case study – London Wetland Centre

Neglected wetlands have been reclaimed at London Wetland Centre, bringing plants and wildlife, including endangered species, back into the local area. Visitors learn about the importance of water as a habitat and how they can help to save water environments.

London Wetland Centre

1. Ducks, geese and swans 2. Adventure area 3. Viewing hide 4. Viewing observatory, with wetlands film 5. Ponds and meadows 6. Reed beds 7. Guided sessions in raised pond area 8. Main lake 9. Partially flooded summer meadow 10. Refreshments.

➤ Action!

Get to know some water near you – for example, a pond, stream or reservoir.

• Visit it regularly and keep a diary of what you see.

• Take photographs.

• List the plants growing there and any animals you see.

Visitors at section 7 in the London Wetland Centre examine a pond and learn about the plants and wildlife that live there.

Challenge!

Become a member or friend of a local body of water such as a wetland centre.

• Your support will help to preserve local water and its plants and wildlife.

Case study – Del Prado Elementary, Florida, USA

More than 200 students, parents and teachers from Del Prado Elementary in Boca Raton, Florida, spent one Saturday bringing the school's pond back to life. The pond had become neglected and some of the wildlife that once lived there had disappeared. To restore it, students collected algae and planted eight species of plants that will attract butterflies, birds and ducks, as well as offer water creatures protection. Throughout the morning, some students raked algae, while others waded into the murky green water to plant duck potatoes, lilies, arrowroot and other plants around the pond's edge.

Lori Paquette, a teacher at Del Prado Elementary, says:

"It's a great way to get kids hooked on environmental science. It's like a little field trip right on your own campus."

Isaac Guido plants a lily in the water as he helps to restore a pond in the grounds of Del Prado Elementary School, Florida.

Ryan Robertson hands his father, Jeff Robertson, a fire flag plant as they help restore a pond in the grounds of Del Prado Elementary School, Florida.

Ice

Most of the fresh water on Earth is locked up in ice. Ice covers three per cent of the Earth's surface. Most of it is at the North and South Poles where the temperature hardly ever rises above freezing.

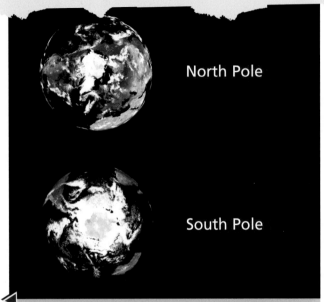

North Pole

South Pole

This photograph shows the extent of the ice caps at the Earth's North and South Poles. This ice is melting rapidly.

Records show that ice is melting in the Arctic at a worryingly fast pace.

Why is ice important?

Ice helps to control the climate all around the world. It reflects heat from the sun away from the Earth and helps to stop the temperature from rising too high.

Melting ice!

Global warming is caused by the effect of too many greenhouse gases such as carbon dioxide in our atmosphere. These gases trap heat, and so warm up the planet and melt the ice caps. If too much ice melts into the sea, sea levels will rise and large areas of land will be flooded. Animals will lose their icy habitats and die.

Challenge!

Choose at least one thing you can do to help stop global warming and save the ice from melting.

- Dress warmly and turn the heating down in winter.
- Dress coolly and turn the air conditioning off in summer.
- Turn off lights and don't leave TVs and other electrical equipment on standby.
- Turn off taps.
- Walk or take the bus when you can, instead of going by car.
- Eat fresh, local food.

Emperor penguins live in the Antarctic, and rely on the icy habitat there to survive.

Local zoos often run schemes where you can adopt an endangered animal such as a polar bear.

Polar regions

The Arctic and Antarctic are the polar regions. The Arctic is the area around the North Pole, where seals swim in the water, polar bears hunt on the ice and arctic terns fly in for the summer. The Antarctic is the area around the South Pole, where whales swim in the ocean and penguins live on the ice.

Saving polar animals

Polar bears hunt on the Arctic ice for seals and fish. Now the ice is melting for longer periods of time in the summer, polar bears have less time for hunting and building up stores of fat in their bodies so they can survive the long winter. Penguins are in danger in the Antarctic. The sea is warming up and killing their food supply, making it harder and harder for them to find food. The key to saving polar bears and penguins is to tackle global warming.

Case study – WWF

The WWF (World Wildlife Fund) is a charity that works locally to protect endangered animals and look after their habitats. It works internationally to encourage governments to change policies and reduce greenhouse gas emissions.

There are several organisations that let you adopt penguins and polar bears. Your money will help the organisations to protect animals and their habitats.

➡ Action!

Contact the WWF or another organisation and find out how you can help to save polar animals.

• For example, schemes let you adopt a penguin or a polar bear yourself, or give one to someone for a birthday present.

Oceans

The oceans that cover 70 per cent of the surface of the Earth are made up of salty sea water. Even though we can't drink the oceans, we need to look after them. Sea water is a vital part of the water cycle. Without it, we wouldn't have water to drink.

Why are oceans important?

Oceans are important because they are part of the water cycle. Like the polar ice caps, they affect the weather all over the world. They are a habitat for all kinds of plants and animals and they support seabirds in the air above them and animals and plants along coastlines. This complex web of life is threatened by global warming, pollution, over-fishing and tourism. Global warming heats up the sea and endangers wildlife specially adapted to living in cold water. Pollution poisons the water and kills plants and animals. Over-fishing will eventually make the fish we catch for food extinct. Tourism can destroy beaches and threaten the natural habitat of animals such as turtles.

Oil spillage

When oil spills into the sea from an oil tanker, it takes a long time to disperse. Thick, black oil washes up onto the beaches. It coats the feathers of seabirds so that they can't fly. Oil floating on the surface blocks out the light and causes sea plants and animals to die.

An oil spill from an oil tanker pollutes the water and kills wildlife, causing problems for years afterwards.

On holiday

Holidaymakers can damage or pollute the oceans worldwide. Responsible holidaymakers can really make a difference to the water in the oceans. They make sure holiday activities such as jet skiing or snorkelling do not disturb wildlife or damage corals or beaches. They always take their litter home.

You can learn about the ocean and its importance while you are on a beach holiday.

Coral reefs

Coral reefs are delicate, living organisms. They are easily damaged. If snorkellers touch the coral, kick up sand or feed the fish, the coral will be damaged. Coral reefs are also threatened by global warming.

Challenge!

Look after the oceans.

- Buy fish that are fished in a sustainable way (a way where their numbers are kept stable).
- Remember, everything you do to conserve water helps.

Action!

Be responsible on the beach.

- Litter – take it home.
- Use biodegradable sunscreen when you go swimming.
- Use sunscreen half an hour before swimming. Oil from your sunscreen floating on the water can block the light and harm plants and animals.
- Don't damage habitats such as coral or rock pools.

Some ocean habitats, such as coral reefs, are incredibly fragile and can be easily damaged by people.

Emergency!

Disasters strike in many different ways. They can be caused by drought, floods, fire, earthquakes, hurricanes or a tsunami. All disasters create emergencies that need a quick response. Getting clean drinking water to the victims of a sudden disaster can mean the difference between life and death.

A teacher dishes up clean drinking water out of a huge metal pot to refugees who lost their homes during the Darfur conflict in Sudan. Fresh water is in short supply.

Emergencies

During an emergency, freshwater supplies are usually affected. Floods cause contamination of drinking water by mixing it with sewage, sea water mud, dirt and rubbish. A big earthquake breaks water pipes and cuts off water supplies. During a war, water supplies are not repaired or looked after. Lack of rainfall during a drought dries up water supplies for people, plants and animals.

 **Action!**

Read newspapers and listen to or watch news bulletins.

• Respond to emergencies.
• Raise money at home or at school for fresh water and sanitation.

Case study – Afghanistan

Drought and the war in Afghanistan have left communities without drinking water and sanitation. Fighting and bombing make it difficult to help people in dangerous, war-torn areas. The organisations UNICEF and USAID and the government of Denmark are working with local people to build and repair wells and toilets, install hand pumps and transport water to remote villages.

Delivering water aid

When disaster strikes, UNICEF responds immediately with supplies of clean water, water purification tablets, re-hydration salts for diarrhoea and water purification equipment. Then long term projects are set up. Hand pumps and new wells are drilled, old wells are mended and toilets and sewage systems are built.

Case study – Pakistan

In October 2005, a catastrophic earthquake hit northern Pakistan. Providing safe water to the millions affected by the disaster was a top priority. Just days after the earthquake, UNICEF set to work repairing water supply systems in Muzaffarabad and other shattered cities, providing safe water to more than 400,000 people. It also helped to repair nearly 200 rural water systems, helping around 700,000 people affected by the disaster.

A boy collects water at a Mark II hand pump provided by UNICEF, near the town of Laghman in Afghanistan.

Children use a water sanitation system set up in Muzaffarabad after the 2005 earthquake.

Children and water

Children everywhere need water for drinking, cooking and keeping clean and for toilets. Without clean water, they cannot stay healthy, grow strong and learn. Children can help each other by saving and looking after water, responding to emergency appeals and by supporting water projects.

Rubbish and garbage collect in a pool of water at a fishing village in Nha Trang, Vietnam.

Sanitation

More than 2 billion people all over the world have no access to toilets or clean water. As a result, diseases such as diarrhoea are spread that can kill young children, old people and others who are weak or ill. Proper sanitation helps to keep people and the environment healthy.

International Year of Sanitation

In September 2000, the United Nations General Assembly signed up to eight Millennium Development Goals in an effort to reduce poverty and increase health and well-being. In 2008, in an effort to speed up the fight against disease, an International Year of Sanitation (IYS) was annouced. The IYS introduced a seven-year plan to halve the number of people without access to basic sanitation.

Challenge!

Find out about IYS, the work of UNICEF and other water charities.

- Find out how you can get involved.
- Raise money with your family and at school.

INTERNATIONAL YEAR OF SANITATION

IYS is supported by UNICEF.

Carol Bellamy, Executive Director of UNICEF says:

"Every primary school in the world should be equipped with separate sanitary facilities for boys and girls and have a source of clean and safe drinking water."

Action!

Read about the Children's World Water Forum and think about how you can help fight for change, too.

- Choose one way of making a difference.
- Find out what progress is being made and make sure something effective is being done. Write letters and send petitions to adults responsible for taking action.

Children

Children who understand the importance of clean water will later teach their own children about it. This way, more and more people will understand and do something about clean water and gradually the situation will improve. The future is in the hands of children.

Case study – Children's World Water Forum

In 2006, the annual Children's World Water Forum, organised by UNICEF, was held in Mexico City. Children from all over the world got together to learn about water, to take action and to get governments to take action. Dolly Akhter, 13, from Pakistan, told the conference how learning about the importance of clean water had meant that her family "always knows about hygiene and being clean, so we don't get sick."

Dolly Akhter with her parents. They are keen that Dolly shares what she has learnt in Mexico with children back home.

Glossary

Chemicals
Chemicals are substances we use for all kinds of things including cleaning, cooking and killing pests. Some chemicals can damage the environment.

Climate change
Climate change is the changing pattern of weather all over the world, caused by global warming.

Contamination
Contamination is another word for pollution. If air, water or soil is contaminated it is made dirty by something that has been added to it.

Dissolve
To dissolve means to break up and mix with water. Oil does not dissolve in water and pollutes it.

Eco-friendly
Eco-friendly means not being harmful to the environment or to the plants and animals that live in it.

Global warming
A rise in the Earth's temperature caused partly by burning oil, gas and coal.

Pollution
Pollution is caused when something harmful goes into water, air or soil. Oil spills from tankers pollute the sea. Exhaust fumes pollute the air.

Sanitation
Sanitation is water supply, toilets and sewage systems. Without good sanitation, people can become ill and the environment may be damaged.

Sustainable fishing
If something is sustainable it can be kept going. Sustainable fishing means fishing in a way that doesn't reduce the number of fish and endanger them.

Water cycle
The water cycle is the movement of water round and round. Rain falls to the ground and runs down into the sea and rivers. Sea and river water evaporates into clouds, and falls again as rain.

Weblinks

http://www.unicef.org/wash/index_31731.html
The participants of the Children's World Water Forum 2006 worked hard on an outcome document they could all be proud of. Read what they had to say.

www.unwater.org/worldwaterday
Learn about World Water Day and join people all over the world in promoting awareness of the importance of clean water and sanitation.

http://www.unicef.org
Find out about the work of the United Nations International Children's Emergency Fund and how they bring water to people in disaster areas.

http://www.wwt.org.uk/visit-us/london
The London Wetland Centre is just one of the WWT wetlands you can visit.

http://www.wwf.org
The World Wildlife Fund is an organisation that protects animals in their natural habitats all over the world. Find out how you can adopt an endangered animal.

http://gowild.wwf.org.uk/gowild
The World Wildlife Fund for kids.

Note to parents and teachers:
Every effort has been made by the Publishers to ensure that these websites are suitable for children, that they are of the highest educational value, and that they contain no inappropriate or offensive material. However, because of the nature of the Internet, it is impossible to guarantee that the contents of these sites will not be altered. We strongly advise that Internet access is supervised by a responsible adult.

Index